DARK ENCOUNTERS

POETIC DARK EXPRESSIONS

BABILUV

DARK ENCOUNTERS

Copyright © 2016 Brandi Ferguson

All rights reserved. No part of this book may be reproduced or transmitted in any form or by any means, electronic or mechanical, including photocopying, recording, or by any information storage and retrieval system, without permission in writing from the publisher. All questions and/or request are to be submitted to: 134 Andrew Drive, Reidsville, NC, 27320.

To the best of said publisher knowledge, this is an original manuscript and is the sole property of author **BRANDI FERGUSON aka BABILUV**

Printed in the United States of America
ISBN-13:978-1537344218
ISBN-10:1537344218

Printed by Createspace 2016
Published by BlaqRayn Publishing Plus 2016

DARK ENCOUNTERS

Dedication

This book is dedicated to anyone who was unable or couldn't use a verbal voice to speak on how they feel. I wrote these poems (which are all based on my feelings) to hopefully help anyone speak, whether it be with their written voice or their spoken voice.

Please read with caution due to the nature of some of the writings. Some of these writing may be triggering for some readers.

Always remember there's someone out there that can feel your exact emotion and understand your feelings. Please don't be afraid to reach out for help.

With love,
Babiluv

DARK ENCOUNTERS

POETIC DARK EXPRESSIONS

BABILUV

DARK ENCOUNTERS

Always

I know what it's like to be an outcast
The one who never finish first but always finish last
I know what it's like to be bullied
Always known as a gothic rocking a black hoody
Always walked with a chip on my shoulder and always moody

Although I always had my reason
My "friends" all committed treason
Lost all respect for those I thought I trust
For a moment I gave up on love and lust
My attitude always portrayed me as being rude
My personality was of a real dude
Slapping high fives and giving daps
Never one to hug, none of that
If I felt a man violated

My first thought will be he must be castrated
If a girl ever tested my knowledge
My fist would make her spit words only used in college
My raw material would leave your words inexplicable
With my vocabulary you only understand minimal
Even if I spoke in plain English you wouldn't get the criteria
Are you even catching this trivia?
I'm the nerd with the sickest flow

DARK ENCOUNTERS

All I can do is explore and grow
Reading books is very fundamental
Haven't yet reached my fullest potential
These words I ink aren't accidental
Imma stop for now and put this on an instrumental

Belief

I ink to write the pain away
Trying to leak out the hurt, in my heart is where it stays
Trying to turn this grey into a sunny day
Clouds opening catching all my hidden fears
Elaborating on how this life really grinds my gears
Looking for answers from an invisible guy
Can't believe in something you can't see with the naked eye
But some gotta believe in something
Others believe in nothing
Not one to claim to be atheist
Yet not one to confess to a priest
I own up to my actions and consequences to say the least
Some say 666 is the sign of the beast
Others say one day the gates of hell will open and demons will be released
I, on the other hand just want the world to be at some type of
peace

Busy Tone

Busy tone is all you hear when I'm on the phone
Forget call waiting I'm not in the mood to hear your tone
I just want to be left alone
My high been past blown
The anger in my eyes can be shown
The angry tears streak down my pretty face
Inner rage makes me want to put you in your place
Blood from biting my lip is what I taste
I have to get out of here before I do damage
Not like Hulk Hogan but more like Randy Savage
Mind pulling me to do evil things
I feel uncontrolled wit these devil's wings
Hoping these feelings is only for the moment
Believe me I try not to do these evil deeds with enjoyment
But my heart wants you to feel my pain
Ideas of locking you down with heavy chains
Scattered thoughts about whether I should torture
But I'm set on already torching her
My hands have a mind of their own
As I chainsaw you to the bone
See I told you, you should've left me the fuck alone

They Say

Why does one have faith and hope?
Why can't our natural chemicals allow us to cope?
Forcing religion on me won't work, nope
How can I have a feeling when all I feel is emptiness?
Lately, feeling the dreary of hopelessness
There are no words that can compare to how I feel
Sometimes I wonder if this is really the deal
Constantly hearing let Jesus take the wheel
They say he comes and presents miracles and heal
Well where is he at? I have words I need to spill
My anxiety gets so high that I must take this pill
At times I am so numb
I can't even feel the pinch of my thumb
Where's all this emptiness coming from?
Screams of get it together blasts my ear drum
At times I can't even hear myself hum
My mania slows down and depression enters my soul
Desperately trying to sew up my torn heart's hole
But soon those stitches will break and I'll be back to square one
Trying to keep hope alive but I'm temporarily done

Cardiac Arrest
(Second Chance)

Went into cardiac arrest at 23
Crossing the street and a car was speeding
I lay passed out bleeding
I remember my fiancée asking am I alright
But something was wrong with my eyesight
Damn why I come to Staten Island tonight?
Only to get some shoes so I can party
But now I was breathing but, hardly
I went pulse less
I only saw darkness
Woke up from the chest compressions
With a paramedic asking me questions
But they can't hold my attention
I knocked back out
But I could hear what they were talking about
They were calling in to the hospital
They didn't think it was possible
To save my life, I can hear it all
I didn't even get to be a mother or wife
Thoughts process in my head
Meanwhile thinking imma be dead
I woke up later in an ICU bed
I was intubated but, I made it
Had a broken nose, teeth, fractured cheekbone
And a torn ACL
My face was unrecognizable

DARK ENCOUNTERS

The thoughts I had would make you think its imaginable
The healing process took time
But not as long as it took to heal my mind
But I survived, being revived
My second chance has arrived

Creativity

Sometimes I feel all alone in my gifted mind
My words urge to be spoken, not hide
I want people to hear my unique perspectives
I want them to listen without objections
But my words aren't able to be spoken
They lie on this paper unspoken
Who would want to hear the mind of a delusional brain?
Who constantly wants to hear about agony and pain?
Our brain is set on one path, or so we're trained
But even the brain can derail
The mind certainly can be frail
It can be dehydrated from lack of well being
But only the core is what everyone is seeing
The mind that can play tricks on you
Making you believe you can't accomplish whatever you can do
You hesitate before every action
Scared that your work won't be satisfaction
You try not to depend on people with your life problems
You think there's no help so you yourself must solve them
Trying to piece the maze in your head
While trying to keep one foot ahead
You want to be the leader everyone is talking about
But all you can think about is the dooming doubt

DARK ENCOUNTERS

Your overactive negative neutrons bring negativity
As you try to push through and enter positively
Hey, they always say, the twisted minds have the most creativity

Death Calling

Please help her with this travesty
Another life lost due to tragedy
Unfortunately she couldn't find another strategy
Her mind was set up already
Committing acts with her mind unsteady
But, death was calling so she got ready
Applying makeup with a hint of lip gloss
Battling with life just to realize she lost
Sinking into the bathtub with sleeping pills in her hand
If someone could have helped her stand
Maybe life would have been grand
But now she sinks below the water like quick sand
Pills slowly taking effect
Too late to regret
Suicide letter left on the bed
The water is now over her head
Her mind slipping away from her body
Her last thoughts of thinking she's a nobody
She allows death to take her last breath
Leaving her soul to finally rest

DARK ENCOUNTERS

Emotion

Raving emotions that come from minute to minute
Racing thoughts with mind blowing ideas behind it
When will this roller coaster of madness alleviate?
Depression rolls into mania and then it will disintegrate
Medications slowly destroying what makes you feel great
Not knowing what your next move is so you just sit and wait
Yet insomnia creates a genius of art and pain
Even a lobotomy couldn't make this maniac sane
Ideas needed to be put on paper comes out utterly insane
Unable to feel a worthy enough emotion
Mania seem to be a better off promotion
Than these sad tears that need a permanent demotion
Yet you still have this outstanding devotion
To continue with your everyday notion
The self action you can not resist
No matter how much mania exist
Moods may vary but addiction will always co-exist

Endless Thoughts

Sleepless nights causes distant thoughts
That brings around all that haunts
Whispers and ghastly taunts

DARK ENCOUNTERS

Closing your eyes won't steer you away from the terror
No matter where you mentally run it won't leave you, never
It's like a tumor attached to a much needed organ
Like adapting to something in you that is foreign
Rapid thoughts won't allow you to concentrate thoroughly
You can feel your world spiraling down hurriedly
Seem to be surrounded by a black hole of emptiness
Down into a pit that seems to go on and on, endless
Comforting yourself within mixed mania and sorrow
Half thoughts of wondering will you be there tomorrow
If only there was another soul you can temporarily borrow

Flatline

As you press your ear to my chest, you listen
You hear no heartbeat, it's missing
The echo of hollowness is what you hear
You begin to think there's something wrong with your ear
My pulse has been replaced
In its lonely place
Emptiness fills this dark place
My heart turned out to be a waste
Frozen then shattered
Badly bruised and battered
Stepped on and splattered
My heart is beyond broken
No longer praying or hoping
Unable to cooperate with coping
Everyone around begins to slowly stray
Anger in my heartless soul is where my emotions stay
Can't shake this coldness away
Will this go on every single day?
Ran out of words, mute on what to say

DARK ENCOUNTERS

Invisible Chains

I need someone to save me
A hero to alter my mentality
Someone to prevent me from causing a fatality
Anyone who can help me not become a casualty
A casualty of my inner being
One to stop this pain from ever beginning
A life where there's forgiving
To erase the battling scars I hold within
No longer wanting to harbor these emotions yet again
Wanting to free my soul without feeling it burning my skin
Stopping this starvation just to be thin
Faking a smile just to fit in
I need an equal that won't make me change
Someone who won't leave me when I become deranged
One who won't keep me locked down in these invisible chains

Trying to Live

Trying to deal with her demented twisted mind
Constantly reliving the past, brain on automatic rewind
Demons and angels seems to be entwined
Trying to survive and not become a chalked outline

DARK ENCOUNTERS

Her promiscuous ways lead her to look for the love she can't find
Her thoughts are of constant wails and a pitching whine
Hearing ghostly whispers that is impossible to contain
Positive thoughts get harder and harder to retain
Demons eating at her heart yet she tries to maintain
Desperately trying to maintain her composure
Trying not to let anyone know her issues, trying to prevent exposure
But the feeling of doom seems to get closer and closer
She's tired of this up and down roller coaster
Battling with the delusional noises that wreck her brain
Trying to have a one way path but it's too late for her mind to be retained
Mental illness is once again to be blamed

Modern Day Edgar Allen Poe

Modern day female version of Edgar Allen Poe
Poetry similar to his sadistic and horror flow
Writing demented gory poetry that's worse than
The Black Cat
Twisted bipolar mind with creativity, imagine that
Enjoying the darkness and gruesome words of Tale
Tell Heart
Inspiring me to openly write gothically from the
start
Reading the poem The Raven
Had me artistically craving
For my pen to be demonically lethal
Reading these horrific tales can lead you to run to a
steeple
Indulging in my writings can leave you deeply
disturbed
Complicated word play can leave you slightly
perturbed
Reading these wicked writings will make you think
I'm out of my mind
In my book of tales, twisted horror is what you may
find
Writing about death, tragedy and doom
Always seem to circle my thoughts and loom
Daughter of darkness with an appetite for lost souls
that's bottomless
These metaphors will leave you utterly breathless

Trying to piece together these corroded thoughts
leaves me restless

Contagious Dark Words

I'm known as a dark deep poet
You'll be sucked into my words without even knowing it
Hypnotizing you casing an epilepsy fit
These words lift off paper like it has a life of its own
My writings could give you nightmares, you should never read alone
If these words could speak you would hear a devilish tone
Taunting your thoughts as you try to erase what you have read
It's too late my contagious words are already wrapped inside your head
Seeping into the sutures of your brain
The noise of doom sounding loud like a construction crane
All this commotion begins to leave your mind mentally drained
My demonic poetry left your once warm heart cold and maimed
There's no turning back now, there's no way for this illusion to be tamed

DARK ENCOUNTERS

My Best Friend

Can't shake the depression that is creeping in
Why must this happen again and again
Looks like depression is becoming my best friend
Waiting for me to meet I wish I could borrow
Playing Russian Roulette with these different type of sorrows
Mental pain that I've become accustomed to
If only people around me knew
The many ill feelings that are beginning to spew
My true depressive mood is only shown to very few
This battle makes me weaker the more it occurs
The more it comes the more I begin to concur
That this depression is encoded into my DNA strand
Not one to reach for an open stranger's hand
The more it cripples me the harder it is to stand
Crying doesn't mend the wound of a shot down heart
Constantly waiting for this depression to finally depart
But it's like a leech that been sucking me dry from the start
Becoming immune to the consequences of the sadness
Just trying to save myself from going into complete madness

DARK ENCOUNTERS

My Fate

I feel trapped like a fly caught in a spider web
Feeling bloated like I'm being forced fed
Looking into the mirror, my eyes look dead
"Stress is a killer" is a quote I once read
With that being said
Why can't I get these sinful thoughts out of my head?
My heart is feeling as heavy as led
Sometimes waking up the next day is a dread
Gets harder and harder to get out of bed
I wear this mask to disguise
My face and the expression of lies
The pain behind these eyes I try so hard to hide
Keep emotions bottled up inside
Never one to ask for help since I have too much pride
My pulse beats with a burning sensation, fried
The innocence in me has already cried
Left with only emptiness
What's life without happiness?
Misery loves company, that shit contagious
My conscious left leaving my brain spacious
Beginning to lose touch with reality, dissociate
Brain shooting blanks like a man unable to procreate
Who's not to say this present life is my ultimate fate

DARK ENCOUNTERS

My Mind

All I feel is chaos in my mind
Look and you shall find
This brain mangled
Unable to be untangled
Fucked up in all angles
What made my mind go into shambles?
They say God only gives you what you can handle
I don't believe and toss the bible off the mantle
Feeling the shadow of demons looming over my soul
Then wonder why I am so cold
It's hard carrying this heavy load
Just want to climb the highest mountain and explode
Scream the demons out of my throat
Trying not to give up and lose all hope

The Path

The urge and desire to feel pain
All hopes of happiness swirled down the drain
How can she refrain from this urge?
How to resist this purge to indulge
Swallowed in pitch of darkness
Never thought the end would feel like this
Sitting in the bathtub with slit wrist
Closing her eyes, she won't be missed

DARK ENCOUNTERS

Her path was chosen regardless
Getting help felt useless
Her life felt needless
Only if she knew her poetry left people speechless
She couldn't see that her life wasn't meaningless
As the blood leak she asks for forgiveness
Her pain went unnoticed, oblivious

No Desire

Her will to live is no longer
The urge to die only gets stronger
The hopelessness is becoming too much to bear
Giving up on everyone, even if they seem to care
Her dying written voice is what she's desperately trying share
Anxiety that rise makes her want a quick demise
No one can understand the dark pain that's within her eyes
Leaving permanent scars to be seen carelessly
Not caring as people look on as she walks around aimlessly
No desire to continue with this life mindlessly
In the mirror she doesn't see what everyone else see
Pleading with her own soul to finally be set free
Conflicting thoughts try to mask her true identity
Living this life with borderline personality
Her actions are whose responsibility?
Dissociating for her own personal protection
Scared to give off the slightest bit of affection
A master at severe self-destruction
With a mind that's constantly under construction

Questions

I prevented writing about you dad
I am angry and I am so mad
But I have this other emotion called sad
Tears drip down my face
My emotions are all over the place
Why did you take your motorcycle to see grandma?
Why didn't you just take your car?
Now you're in a coma and my thought s remain far
My feelings are all detached
My heart can't be reattached
Did I say I love you when I called you back?
Controlling my emotions is something I lack
I can't apologize for the past
Everything happened so fast
Three weeks ago on my birthday is when I heard your
voice last
I close my eyes and reenact your crash
Feeling somehow it's my fault
Your life is now at a halt
Only 49 years old
You're too young to leave this world
What about your 8 year old little girl?
I hurt more for her
Can't imagine the pain she'll endure
Or what about my son Ayden?
He doesn't understand right now but he's waiting
We all waiting for you to open your eyes

DARK ENCOUNTERS

They say you'll be the same, but I know those are lies
I can't have faith you'll return to me
It's hard to believe in something I can't see

Tension
TRIGGER WARNING

They say reach out when you feel like this
But it's hard to reach out when you have slit wrist
This knife was calling and screaming out to me
Wanting me to slice my skin and set my blood free
Too much anxiety and too many urges
All these thoughts make me wanna purge
To temporarily release all this unwanted tension
Everyday the thoughts become an extended extension
Waiting to leave this universe isn't a tough decision
Closing my eyes and seeing blood leak from me is what I vision
I rather these thoughts vanish, that's all I'm wishing

My Curse

Sometimes I feel like I'm going through a curse
Although I know things can be much worse
Most of the time I walk and don't have peripherals
Not wanting my unstable emotions to be visible
Sometimes I do wish to be invisible
Pray, is that what he and she said

DARK ENCOUNTERS

Am I seeing hell? Cuz when I close my eyes all I see is red
This pain can't seem to cease no matter how much I've bled
Trying to get these tormented thoughts outta my head
At times it's hard to get out of the bed
How much more of this can I handle?
So angry that sometimes I want to knock out someone's mandible
I see I need to set my own vigilance candle

The Cut
TRIGGER WARNING

Self-infliction is definitely my despairing addiction
I love the very first affliction
Every scar every addition
Every cut marks my flesh
With every cut my life is expressed
The love to feel pain makes me obsessed
This blade cuts deep and I like it, I must confess
I cut with whatever is available
Rusty box cutters, razors and pocket knives litter my table
I close my eyes and let the blood flow
I release the pain in my mind and let it all go
I'm left with horrific scars to show
If able I would cut everyday to my sanity
These thoughts are embedded in me for eternity
Scars of my life written on my legs and arm
I don't care for opinions, yes I self harm
I don't pay attention to the stares or the glares
You can't judge my life it just isn't fair
Permanent marks on my body are like a map
Each slice is for a different mishap
Can't let go of this habit, I feel trapped
I used to cry for help but what was the use
I cannot ever be changed; I am not a blown fused
My thoughts of self harm can never be diffused
As I get older I get more confused

DARK ENCOUNTERS

As a mother I feel I need to improve
But the thoughts of self harm are unmoved
Seventeen years of the same action
Eighteen hospitalizations for this reaction
When will it end?
Seem like self harm is my best friend

The Dark Poet

I'm known as a dark deep poet
You'll be sucked into my words without even knowing it
Hypnotizing you causing an epilepsy fit
These words lift off this paper like it has a life of its own
My writings could give you nightmares, you should never read alone
If these words could speak you would hear its devilish tone
Taunting your thoughts as you try to erase what you have read
It's too late my contagious words are already wrapped inside your head
Seeping into the sutures of your brain
The noise of doom sounding loud like a construction crane
All this commotion begins to leave your mind mentally drained
My demonic poetry left your once warm heart cold and maimed
There's no turning back now, there's no way for this illusion to be tamed

Urges

The urges to self mutilate has returned
You would have thought after the last time I would've learned
I guess those 4 stitches did nothing to satisfy my greed
But this knife to my skin begins to bleed
Nothing can divert my attention, not even this weed
One day I'll cut too deep and the blood poring out would leave me
in a coma-like sleep
So tired of hearing my inner being weep
My sanity I can't seem to grasp and keep
The feeling of being agitated and frustrated
Marks on my arms and legs hideously illustrated
The length of my depression has already been demonstrated
My life story is something no one would want to plagiarize
Feeling how I feel you would want those thoughts vaporized
Not schizophrenic but I occasionally hear these menacing voices
Telling me you're not allowed to make to make your own choices
Pressing me to deal with these raw emotions
Emotions that I'm not ready to face
Cowardly thinking if I go head to head with myself it'll be a waste

DARK ENCOUNTERS

My body became accustomed to the blood taste
But once I start this cycle I'm unable to stop
One day my artery might just pop
But then it'll be too late and my body will drop

DARK ENCOUNTERS

The Hurt

The hurt in my heart is so real
These life events are so surreal
Too much going on, how can I deal?
No longer able to process positive thoughts
These demons relentlessly possesses me and continues
to haunt
Whispering things won't get better so they consistently taunt
Sometimes I feel like this curse is my fault
My feelings have all came to a screeching halt
My anger has transformed to being numb
If a truck ran me over the pain would be nil to none
Can't feel shit, not even a sore thumb
My life is like a Russian Roulette only instead it's with
a loaded gun
Each bullet piercing my organs waiting for death to come
Desperately trying to escape but I can't run
Nightmares killing me slowly until my devastated soul is done

DARK ENCOUNTERS

The Listening Demon

Gross and abnormal fatalities emerges like fantasies in her head
She feels consoled with the demon like it's a teddy bear in her bed
She rather expresses her demonic thoughts with the demon instead
She shows him all the places she's constantly bled
The demon just sits and actively listens
Listening to all the gore as its eyes glistens
Ingesting her words as though it's his breakfast
Allowing her to act out on negative thoughts, he's relentless
She continues to pour out her soul until she becomes breathless
The demon now begins to smile
She's now in trouble for becoming so senile
He's been after her soul this whole while

RUN

Running through the wild in desperation
The woods hear your shallow respiration
The scary whispers of the trees leave no inspiration
Your body is soak and wet from severe perspiration
Looking back can cause unnecessary devastation
Death seem to have made you a V.I.P reservation
Wanting to capture your soul for self preservation

DARK ENCOUNTERS

At any minute your heart can explode, that's observation
Trying to out run death with strong determination
Yet death laughs knowing soon you'll be on your way to termination

The Urge

The urge is back
The wanting of satisfying this beast within
The wanting to use this blade and cut this skin once again
When am I ever going to learn?
Learn to deal with emotions without having to feel the burn
The burn of release, blood seeping from my flesh
Needing to see something recent, something fresh
Wanting to reopen physical scars
Want to feel something real without wishing upon stars
To feel the rush, the adrenaline
To feel the power, masculine
Can't seem to get out of the depressive state I'm in
Can these self destructive acts really be an unforgivable sin?

Assuming

Running away is her natural instinct
Emotions since young became extinct
Mental blockage leaves her unable to think
Moods can switch before she can even blink
She loves to gaze up at the stars and moon

Wondering if she's going to meet up with her lost loved
ones soon
Unable to voice her inner expressions
People just assume she's going through depression

Unable

Unable to speak my emotions so I write with this pen
Unable to process neither my thoughts nor the predicament I'm in
Living a lie and trying to rid my sins
But I repent if I repeat the same sins again
Calling me crazy
But I say mentally deranged
But I can't be changed
After a few words exchanged
Now you calling me strange

The Night

Not a savior in sight
My soul stolen like a thief in the night
Frozen in a delusional universe
Breaking into reality would only be worse
Lifelessly living with a curse
Red is what I see when I close my eyes
Blue isn't the color I see in the skies
Night terrors don't allow be to sleep
Poltergeist seem to come and creep
Got my mind spiraling way too deep
Mood changes more than a mood ring
Devils scream, I never hear the angels sing
Dreaming of an angel to take me under its wing
Heart swollen like a person allergic to a bee sting
I try to wake up like this reality is just a dream
But I'm forever in this nightmare it seem
I want the life I read about in a magazine
Picket fence with dark green grass
But even if I escaped, how long would it last?

Thoughts

Suicidal thoughts again swimming around in my cerebrum
I try and try but can't seem to even temporary erase them
These thoughts aren't the only inhuman but worrisome
It's like I'm anticipating for my death to finally come
I wonder if at my last breath would I still be numb
Would I feel the pain and know where the pain is coming from
Different possibilities enter my mind when thinking about suicide
These possessive thoughts cause my brain to override
Overriding the positive thoughts that try desperately to slip through
Misery loves company, this may be true
But I much rather suffer alone
Not wanting to hear others chastising tone
Screaming why won't these thoughts leave my head
Why when I'm a mother I would want to see myself dead
I'll just live with my soulless empty feeling life instead

Low

Stuck in a place where I feel numb
Insecurities like a newborn sucking her thumb
Feeling down, lower than my town's bum
Hate when my plays tricks, feeling like a scum
I drown my feelings with this Bacardi Rum
These obstacles are getting so hard to overcome
But I continue to move to the beat of this drum
Feelings of joy? I feel none
Moods switching like transmission gears
Patronizing is all I ever hear
Your hurtful words cause bleeding in my ear
Having a provoked blackout is something I fear
No warmth is left to feel once you come near
Life on the surface isn't what it all appears
Feeling like I just want to disappear
Heart struck by an Indian spear
Hard to survive in the lack of space I have here

DARK ENCOUNTERS

Trapped Alone

Trapped inside this body with a tortured soul that's eager to reappear
Yet the other personality desperately wants her soul to disappear
Waiting and waiting for death to come somewhat near
She's ready to face death and no longer have any fear
She's tired of the broken promises and the lying
So she sleeps and dreams about the day she is dying
Tired of reaching out to imaginary help
No one hears the suicidal voice in her yelp
Painting a happy mask on her face is no longer working
The grim reaper is over her head, constantly lurking
Her lost soul is weak and way beyond repair
She lives everyday with constant despair
The world is so cold and so unfair
So she weeps as this blade releases her pain
Trying to figure out whether she's really insane
This knife against her skin temporarily makes life worth living
Although she knows her demons are unforgiving
Watching the blood leak from her arms gives her satisfaction
Oblivious to every other person's facial reaction
This gives her a temporary satisfying distraction
Her marked up body looks like a circus attraction

She feels so alone yet she knows her death is set in stone
There's nothing to be done once she's entered the death zone
She wants to pray but heaven won't answer the phone
Even when she tries to reach hell she gets no dial tone
She soon realizes that even in death she'll be all alone

DARK ENCOUNTERS

Stuck

Stuck in a place where I feel numb
Insecurities like a newborn sucking its thumb
Feeling down, lower than my town's bum
Hate when my mind plays tricks, feeling like scum
Drown my feelings with this Bacardi Rum
These obstacles are getting harder to overcome
But I continue to move to the beat of this drum
Feelings of joy? There are none
Moods switching like transmission gears
Patronizing is all I ever hear
Your hurtful words causes bleeding in my ear
Having a provoked blackout is something I fear
No warmth is left to feel once you come near
Life on the surface isn't what it all appears
Heart striked by an Indian spear
Hard to survive in the lack of space I have here

Where to Go From Here

The thoughts I have will leave me in purgatory
My brain would be left for a scientist to dissect in a laboratory
Waves of senseless thoughts fill my mind
Images far from even being kind
My soul feel like its long have died
Robotic movements to keep active in life

DARK ENCOUNTERS

Going through the motions of being a mother and a wife
Steadily looking for more
But the rain instead steadily pour

DARK ENCOUNTERS

Evilness

Evil souls enters you with raw penetration
Harsh like anal sex with no lubrication
They enter without permission, without an explanation
They already own your heartless soul
Cramped inside like too many fish in a fish bowl
Evilness drowns you into a deep dark hole
It heats your body, setting it on fire
Your sinful soul is what it desire
Angels on strike, not able to hire
Demons take you to the unknown
They take you only, you're all alone
Ghouls creep up beside you and begin to moan
You try not to look at the emptiness of its eyes
Hypnotized as the demon begins to rise
You're fixed on its massive size
Pain shoots through your chest
Too late to pray, your soul is not blessed
All you can do is scream at your best

Feelings in the Cranium

My cranium feel like it's swimming in water
I'm a person, someone's wife mother and daughter
But my mind isn't programmed to this, it's programmed to slaughter
Visions in my head of a bloodbath I want to shed
Is it a sin to want people dead?
You don't read between the lines so this story is unread
Waking up to this horrendous world is a dread
Can't count the many times I've bled
My pen inks blood on this paper
Psychologist examine this brain, they conclude they can't help her
Blackouts and nightmares still occur
What more can come out of this open door?

Casualty of the Pen

Soul painfully damaged and beyond repair
Evil spirits enter my heart, one heart we share
Wanting to live and love life without a care
This turmoil of emotions I'm unable to bare
Can't bare the consequences of these committed sins
All I can do is drown my repents with this gin
Cycle repeats itself again and again

I sit waiting for the repercussions to begin
My life is a beginning without an end
Came into this world alone, Why the fuck do i need a friend?
This is a harsh reality for some people's mentality
This brain is increasingly haunted by thoughts of mortality
Excuse my lack of hospitality
But my pen just committed casualty

Night Terrors

Night terrors haunt my sleepless dreams
Demons sit hard on my chest, unable to breathe it seems
It sits on my chest inhaling the slight air coming from my lips
I'm in a catatonic state unable to move my hips
It slithers to my ear and I hear it hiss
Whispers evil words into my ear
At this moment I wished to be Helen Keller, unable to hear
The growls instills horrific fear
Can't shake this comatose state
I'm just an empty vessel, my soul the demon takes
This vessel sleeps forever unable to awake

DARK ENCOUNTERS

Flesh Eaters

A Lost soul wanders this body
Evil spirits dance in this vessel like a house party
Fragile mind easily damaged
Demons eating at its flesh like a savage
This heart has taken all it can manage
I ink out all this wished carnage
Just me and my paper
Living to wait for a savior?
Can there be a worst hell than living?
Constant repents yet constant sinning
What's the use in prayer when we were doomed from the beginning?
Battle of "heaven" and "hell" yet whose winning?
Real life horror stories must have the devil grinning
I'm so confused, what's the use in believing?

Struggling to Rise

I stare in the mirror and see a complete stranger
Unrecognizable hate and anger
Seething threw my veins, am I in danger?
Cutting myself with the edge of a hanger
Soulless spirits live in this vessel of mine
Whispering sinister thoughts into my mind
Innocence gone like the lost of a girl's virginity
I feel the evil within this vicinity
Lost souls like strippers who dance in sin city

DARK ENCOUNTERS

I don't ask for your sympathy or pity
Permanent scars remind me of my mental struggle
Still trying to rise above the rubble
I'm on my own in this bubble
Not even the sweetest soul can save me from this trouble

Lacking

I suffer from lack of sympathy
Never one to show empathy
My brain not set up like that mentally
Not even physically
My body isn't equip with tear ducks
But I know I don't give 2 fucks
Severely ill tempered
Personality labeled self centered
Can't change myself if I tried
People think I'm nice, someone lied
I can smell a phony a mile away
My intuitions would be considered crazy
I'm a fucking psychic
I know your lie before you even think it
I can sense ignorance
I have no tolerance
Or patience
Been like this since adolescence

The Change

@14 I was already outta my mind
By 16 I was ahead of my time
Constantly trying to find
Where I fit in
Feeling abandoned once again

DARK ENCOUNTERS

Living was an everyday sin
Trust issues couldn't even make a friend
By 18 I thought I reached life's end
Had to be contained
Trying to keep these thoughts maintained
Was gonna give up
Personally I didn't give a Fuck
Felt shit outta luck
Had to change my thought process
Had to do a lot just to progress
Had a lot of growing up to do
So much Shit I'm glad I made it thru
My life far from a dream
Everyday you must believe
Things isn't what it seem
I couldn't go and leave my mother to grieve
Had to think twice
Had to not make that sacrifice
Gotta be here for my son's life

DARK ENCOUNTERS

My Wishes

I wish I could just electrocute you
Decapitate u
Castrate u
Doing things to a 9 yr old u shouldn't do
My lil sis felt the pain too
But I tried to take most of it
And it made me sick
Clung to my sis so she wouldn't be touched
I had to keep hushed
Couldn't have him hurt my sister
At 9 is when I became sinister
By 12 the devil was already in my brain
I was on auto pilot since the 4th grade
Legalized insane
Couldn't do nothing but touch a blade
Then my alter ego was made
Babiluv

The one who did killings without wearing a glove
My hate is for eternity
There's no letting go for me
You never went to jail
But Imma see you in hell

Help Me

Help me rid this evil
Help me become more civil
Help me rid this ice off my heart
Help me get out this dark
Help me apologize
And realize
That I just needed to be recognized
Diagnosed borderline personality
I have trouble dealing with reality
I need you to help me
Help me rid these thoughts of suicide
Help me control these obscene thoughts in my mind
Help me not commit a homicide
I need your assistance
U should know there may be resistance
Help me live in existence
Can u please help me with all this??

DARK ENCOUNTERS

No Sympathy

My words are far from subliminal
I'm a bipolar type criminal
My urges are tough to maintain but, I keep it to a minimal
I'm a raging caged animal
Flesh eating cannibal
Can't wait to get rid of you
Stomp on your corpse then spit on you
No respect for the dead
Unsympathetic that's what the coroner said
Accidental death is what the report read
So disrespectful I go to your wake
I wasn't done, your soul I must take
Like Shang Tsung I need that soul to keep me young and awake

This Anxiety

Anxiety to the max
How can u tell me to relax?
Hiding all these scars
Manic running in between cars
But now the depression set in
Feeling more demons coming in again
I pop this Klonopin
To try and ease my mind
Don't tell me to breath, I've tried/

DARK ENCOUNTERS

Feeling so numb
I can't feel myself hum
Where did this anxiety come from?
I'm so done with all this aching
All this faking
Disaster in the making
Just want to crawl into a corner
I hope my family doesn't have to call the coroner
My heart so scorn
Brain as sharp as a thorn
But this minute now I'm dull
All feelings are null

The Disorders

Pain torn into my heart like piercing bullets
Should feel pain but I'm numb to it
So many times I just feel like letting go and quit
Me living is more disgraceful than someone's spit
Sometimes I just sit and stare completely out of it
Dissociation Identity Disorder
So many diagnosis filed in my folder
Will this continue as I get older?
Got more PTSD than an army soldier
My body is soulless
My mind is mindless
We all gonna die regardless
Mental illness, there's no getting around this
Born with talents of a bipolar artist
Gifted with a slight twist
Dark images swarm, you sure you about this?

My Life

Some of my thoughts can be considered demented
My soul continues to be badly tormented
My inner self burnt to ashes, cremated
My personality is being temporarily renovated
I never understood why I'm so hated
My heart holds pain that's always gated

DARK ENCOUNTERS

Can't get too close I begin to feel suffocated
I black out when arguments become escalated
I hate when people believe my life is fabricated
Feeling like a bullet shattered my brain, fragmented
My heart feel like a ghoul stole it, confiscated
Life is like trigonometry, complicated

The Lows

You feel the depression slowly and painfully
seeping into your body
The acts of self loathing and the constant feeling of
being lonely
Then comes the challenges of getting out the bed
And contemplating on the pros and cons of being
dead
Go to work or jump into a rush hour 5 train?
Debating on speaking up for help as this knife to
your wrist you try to refrain
Refraining from taking a deadly slice as on lookers
watch and become entertained
Most don't understand how hard it is to keep a
suicidal mind contained
Not easy to keep functional but at the same time
life's always been dysfunctional
In a depressive state it's hard for my brain to be
punctual
Purposely dissociating from reality and becoming
absent
Makes people say she doesn't have all her eggs in
one basket
Dull depressive moments turn into gloomy days
Dark room with not a glimpse of a light as I walk
around in a haze
No thought process just a cold brain laying there
restless
The scattered mural on my body would leave you

breathless
Only I know the feeling of being defenseless
The constant feeling of emptiness is beginning to feel relentless
No tears to shed as I swallow into my own protective shell
The secret place my mind and body know so well
The surrounding of silence puts my depressive state under a hidden spell
Mouthing help me I'm trapped but no one can hear
They got tired of the same shit year after year
So, alone you wallow, wallowing into what you fear
Being alone forever or at least until death is near

The Conclusion?

Low and depressive thoughts makes me think the unimaginable
Waiting for something to happen that's magical
But magic is only an illusion
That causes unbelievable confusion
Harsh reality of life with slight delusions
These pills can never substitute for my life's conclusion
Trying to live day by day is very hard for me to say
I can't see any light at the end of this tunnel, there's something in my way
A deeper presence wants me locked away
Stuck in an uncontrollable tormented bubble is

DARK ENCOUNTERS

where I stay
Feel like my mind is being repeatedly abused
Can't categorize these feelings and don't know which one to use
The mix of these moods leave me deeply confused
All these "emotions" and I don't know which to choose
Everything I try to do I always seem to loose
This depression is worst than having the occasional blues
My mind seems to always have a blown fuse
Can't change something that's unable to be diffused

The Toll Of Depression

Can't shake the depression that is creeping in
Why must this happen again and again?
Looks like depression is becoming my best friend
Waiting for me to meet my untimely end
Drowning in sorrow that may not lead to many tomorrows
A happy heart is what I wish I could borrow
Playing Russian Roulette with these different type of sorrows
Mental pain that I've become accustomed to
If only people around me knew
The many ill feelings that are beginning to spew
My true depressive mood is only shown to a few
This battle makes me weaker the more it occurs
The more it comes the more I begin to concur
That this depression is encoded into my DNA strand
The more it cripples me, the harder it is to stand
Not one to reach for an open stranger's hand
Crying doesn't mend the wound of a shot down heart
Constantly waiting for this depression to finally depart
But it's like a leech that's been sucking me dry from the start
Becoming immune to the consequences of this sadness
Just trying to save myself from going into complete madness

DARK ENCOUNTERS

Always Believe

Always numb to the emotion
Moving in slight silence like the ocean
Gotta keep moving, never lose focus
One track mind but you still take notice
No such thing as life ever being smooth sailing
Gotta keep your head high even when you feel like you're failing
Pick your troubles off the floor no matter how far you're trailing
Hard not to let others see your pain, it shows on your face
Obstacles always in place slowing down your quick pace
Gotta slow down, why does life have to be a race?
Writing down your sorrow while thinking about tomorrow
Wishing there's a smile somewhere you can temporarily borrow
Believe life will get better then reread this letter

This Necklace

This cross necklace isn't on my neck due to religion
It's there to protect me from committing all this killing
Keeping me away from all those sinning
I don't preach or try to teach
I don't judge I just keep my thoughts on a tight leash
I have an inner personality waiting to be unleashed
Waiting to be full released
The innocence in me can't be reached
Thirsty demons r out for my soul
They have human faces to mask the ghoul
They drain and manipulate my spirit
The words I speak you wouldn't believe it
Grew up in Catholic Church and believed their lies
Had a hard knock life yet "god" never heard my cries
I gave up which was no surprise
Glimpse of hope will occasionally arise
Who knows what happens when one dies
We rattle our brain trying to forgive and apologize
I'm not gonna even try to rationalize
Some people can't relate
Religion leads to many debates
I'm writing my opinion, don't mistaken it for hate

DARK ENCOUNTERS

In need of a Tourniquet

Someone get a tourniquet for her wrist
She slit them cuz she won't be missed
Her problems were beyond endless
She got stuck out this life
Had to end it with the slice of a knife
She was unable to focus
Feeling life had no purpose
Suicide was the only way out
So young she knew nothing of what life's about
Battling demons that took over her mind
Feelings of depression she so hard tried to hide
Couldn't shake it off no matter how hard she tried
Couldn't release the pain no matter how hard she cried
She thought suicide was best, somebody lied

Trust

My brain is unable to comply with trust
Yet they say trust is a must
Trusting people with my feeling always causes a fuss
I keep my darkest under a lock and key
No one can understand what it's like to be me
Hating when my emotions make me cry uncontrollably
Why can't people just leave me be
Knowing you don't care, you just want to be nosy
But I keep my enemies close and make you believe shit is rosy
I can't trust anyone with how I'm feeling
I can't even concept with what I'm dealing
My mind is like a movie, constantly reeling
Trusting someone with my skeletal closet
No matter how hard I try I can't get over it
The same nightmare occurs as I try to sleep
Depression is only causing me to weep
These sins is what I must try to reap
But I'm in way too deep
My sanity I desperately try to keep
Walking around like the walking dead
Waiting for that speedy bullet to hit me in the head
I feel myself beginning to dissociate
Losing reality, my brain is something you can't locate
This numbness may cause a devastating catastrophe

DARK ENCOUNTERS

Most would think I'm over reacting and my issues are blasphemy
I feel I might snap and not care for the consequences
This horror called life seems to have many sequences
Back to back obstacles that's getting harder to overcome
Where did my depression for life come from?
Heart beating fast like a rhythm of a bass drum
Anxiety taking over my nervous system
They try to force me to take more meds but I fight them
I may be psychotic but I'm never one to be dumb

What To Believe

I ink to write the pain away
Trying to leak out the hurt, in my heart is where it shall stay
Trying to turn this grey into a sunny day
The rain blends in with these weak tears
Clouds opening catching all my hidden fears
Elaborating on how this life really grinds my gears
Looking for answers from an invisible guy
Can't believe in something you can't see with the naked eye
But some have to believe in something
Other believe in nothing
Not one to claim to be atheist
Yet not one to confess to a priest
I own up to my actions and consequences to say the least
Some say 666 marks the sign of the beast
Others say one day the gates of hell will open and demons will be released
I, on the other hand just want the world to be at peace

As Darkness Falls

As Darkness falls, the demon shows their unwanted face

DARK ENCOUNTERS

You try to hide and find a safe place
But they're everywhere, invading your space
You walk around in a haze
Looking for an escape in this demonic maze
Hours turn into infinite days
Trying to evade, while the evil spirits invade
Looking at your soul as a fair trade
Bypassing your vessel cuz its man made
You shiver while being frightened and afraid
You sit and listen to the evil's whispering whistle
Knowing it's better to just end it with a shot of a pistol
You beg for them to disappear
But they smell your endless fear
Too late to resist, they're already near
By your face, licking your lonely tear
As the enter you try to fight
They're too strong and they take you into the dark night
Hoping and praying to see a white light
Your soul steers left but the ghouls pull you right
There's absolutely no escape
You have no choice but to accept your fate

When?

When will there be a smile?
Life's hard but in my shoes can u make it a mile?
Mask my face, living in denial
Can no more tears run down my face
Yet a smile still isn't in place
Depression and anxiety is in a race
One takes over then the other replace
Don't wear my heart on my sleeve, no trace
Happiness tightly thin
Keeping my feelings within
Yet, I feel the negativity coming out my pen
Can't be vulnerable and leave myself open
Words go on this paper, can never be spoken
Words so thick it'll leave one choking
Imma just keep my eyes close and just keep hoping

No Faith

Soulless eyes stare out into the world
Hard to imagine the pain of a hopeless girl
Lack of faith and lack of hope
She hides as the darkness of souls begin to elope
No one to trust with her voice or a single thought
Her past creeps and continues to haunt

DARK ENCOUNTERS

Looking for the light at the end of this dark tunnel
The hurt and pain comes in a starving bundle
How can one even try to handle?
Death begins to light a vigilance candle
Ghouls of life quickly eat like a famished mammal
Flesh eating savages more like a cannibal

ABOUT THE AUTHOR

As a teen, I always knew I had an urge to write. My idol was Edgar Allen Poe and I was intrigued by the darkness in his poetry and short stories.

Diagnosed bipolar at the age of 14, my creative mind began writing down my troubles and feelings into journals. Soon those writings turned into poetry. Never really fitting in with the popular crowd in school, I learned to detach myself from the real world and enter a world of dark poetry.

My unique writings eventually caught the attention of poets on social media as I got older. I always believed writing is in my blood and my creative ink won't stop until my heart does.

Author Brandi "Babiluv" Ferguson

Made in the USA
Columbia, SC
31 October 2017